The Nature of Hearts

Stories of Observation
and Connection

Delila Olsson

The Nature of Hearts:
Stories of Observation and Connection

Published by Wisdom of Nature Press

Paperback: 979-8-9863551-3-9

Hardcover: 979-8-9863551-2-2

Every attempt has been made to properly source all quotes and attribute all research.

Printed in the United States of America

First Edition

Contents

I dedicate this book to my ancestors, who cultivated an open heart and attentive spirit in me. May their legacy live on in the stories to come.

Introduction

The Subtle Art of Seeing

As an educator, I always look forward to summertime—for pleasure reading, reconnecting with friends, puttering in the garden. This year, I had grand plans to tackle some big home projects, visit the ocean, and start a workout routine. But life had other ideas.

Instead, I found myself confined by unexpected health challenges, my body dictating the pace. As inflammation swelled, so did my emotions as I contemplated life in this troubled country and world. As summer slipped away, frustration gave way to reflection. I used my journal to process my thoughts and observations.

Amidst the stillness, I reconnected with memories of walks with my ma and gardening with Gram, the ones who first modeled deep observation and the importance of nurturing growth in all its forms. I could almost feel my fingers sinking into the rich earth, while helping Gram transplant seedlings. The scent of tomato vines and sunshine enveloped us. As we worked, she'd share stories of farming back in Minnesota, where careful watching meant the difference between a thriving crop and a failed harvest. Little did I know, these moments were planting seeds that would blossom into my own lifelong passion for the natural world.

I discovered Montessori education at twenty-one and almost immediately recognized it as my life work. My first job interview included a three-hour silent observation of a classroom filled with 3-6 year olds. I noticed the calm environment, the children deeply engaged in various activities, and a teacher who moved among them without disruption. Kindness, respect, empathy—these were the foundations. Forty years later, this remains my calling.

In Montessori, observation serves a dual purpose. Adults use it to understand each child's needs and the community as a whole. Children, in turn, cultivate observation to classify the impressions their absorbent minds take in. This concept of being both observer and observed struck me profoundly. I remember a five-year-old named Dale who, amidst a heated argument with friends, chose to sit alone on the playground. When I asked if she needed help rejoining the game, she replied, "No thank you. Sometimes it's good to watch for a while." Her self-awareness astonished me, reinforcing the power of quiet attention.

Observation, I've learned, is more than watching others. It is a study of self, an inquiry into why we matter and how we can make a difference. Observation is not just for teachers or children; it's a valuable tool for all humans. It helps us better understand the world and discover the roots of our beliefs by examining our perspectives. In times of division, as we face global challenges bigger than any one of us, mindful attention might help us see a larger perspective than we can individually. Perhaps it could even become a mechanism for bridging what divides us.

My grandparents were my first teachers, showing me the value of learning through quiet, attentive watching. They taught me to understand plants by feeling their roots beneath the soil, to anticipate weather patterns by watching birds. In blackberry patches, I learned to spot giant spiders within thorny branches, working carefully around their webs. These lessons connected me to nature and instilled a profound understanding: while I am important, my life is not more valuable than others.

This is why I journal daily, processing life's experiences, connecting personal challenges to global issues. Reflecting upon the core experiences that set me on my path has helped me rediscover how perspective can transform my state of being. And how the most important lessons of early life continue to guide me into my elder years.

Perhaps the unsettledness in the world stems, in part, from a collective avoidance of life's ugly or complex aspects, as we shy away from what seems unchangeable. Yet if we pause to observe what's happening around and within us, we may discover an opportunity to shift. This heightened awareness can lead to a deeper connection with ourselves and others, revealing the interconnectedness of all things.

The impulse to comfort a friend in pain is the same force driving movements for democracy and equality—a fundamental human desire for connection and understanding. By embracing this awareness, we can recognize that our individual actions ripple outward, affecting the collective whole.

As we navigate life's paradoxes—isolation and connection, fear and hope—we uncover a powerful truth: our shared vulnerability is our greatest strength. This realization fosters a sense of unity, encouraging us to face challenges together rather than in isolation, and to address the complexities of our world with compassion and collective action.

This collection, "The Nature of Hearts," emerged from a summer of introspection. It's a tapestry of my observations and reflections, rooted in a search for clarity and healing. Written during an election year marked by collective unwellness, these essays reflect our profound need for nurturing—both as individuals and as a society. Many will relate to this longing to connect to a story that is bigger than any one of us, viewing the world through personal experience to understand collective issues and our potential impact.

These essays represent what I was able to accomplish, when some days, all I could do was eke out a few words on the page. They're filled with stories of my mother and grandmother, whose spirits I called upon for love and guidance in this writing process. As you will see in this book, they showed up for me as our ancestors tend to do: when we ask.

I offer these stories, my contribution to life's grand narrative, with gratitude. May they serve as a reminder of the healing power of nature, the importance of nurturing ourselves and others, and the transformative potential of careful observation in these challenging times.

The Nature
of Hearts

The Nature of Hearts

In life, we often find what we seek, our attention acting as a divining rod for meaning. I've become an accidental collector of hearts, guided by the mysterious workings of observation and perception.

More than four decades ago, a heart-shaped rock tucked inside a letter from Matt, a young man I loved, became the first piece in my collection. Our summer romance, brief but intense, unfolded mostly through correspondence while he was away on an archaeological dig. That first stone spoke to me of omens and possibilities.

Years later, on the sands of Point Roberts, Washington, another heart emerged from the Earth. In a moment of personal angst, I had cast a silent plea into the universe. The response came not as a whisper, but as a perfectly formed stone at my feet—a tangible answer to an intangible question.

Suddenly, I began to notice hearts everywhere—in rocks, leaves, and shadows. Each discovery became a reminder of that initial surge of hope, a thread connecting me to something larger than my immediate struggles. These stone hearts evolved into a currency of connection, and I've often passed them on as tokens of my affection. Friends have brought me hearts from around the Earth—Machu Picchu, Mount Shasta, the coasts of Maine and Scotland—each carrying the essence of its origin, a piece of the world's vast tapestry.

In 2007, while digging through a trunk of childhood memorabilia, I rediscovered that first rock from Matt. This led to an unexpected reconnection, made more poignant by the discovery that Matt had recently received a heart transplant. The synchronicity was striking—a stone heart from the past resurfacing as Matt received a brand new, beating heart. This rediscovery sparked a brief rekindling of romance, established a lifelong friendship, and reminded us that love's essence persists beyond time and circumstance.

These heart-shaped wonders in nature become messengers of a universal pulse. The ivy's unfurling leaf, the delicate bloom of the bleeding heart flower, the hidden chamber within a walnut—all echo the rhythm that beats within our own chests, speaking to our innate desire for connection and our yearning to feel part of something greater.

While these encounters could be dismissed as mere coincidence, I've come to see them as invitations to deeper awareness. They are symbolic whispers, urging us to look closer, to recognize the threads of love and connection woven through the fabric of our lives.

And so, when I stumble upon a moss-covered rock bearing the silhouette of a heart or step over a cordate seed pod, I am reminded of love's persistence. It is always there, waiting to be discovered, if we have the eyes to see and the heart to recognize it.

Blessed:
A Legacy of
Resilience

Blessed: A Legacy of Resilience

Resilience is the ability to adapt to adversity and stress, to flex when things don't go as we imagine they will. In times of difficulty or uncertainty, emotional resilience keeps one tethered to hope rather than despair.

Children learn essential skills of resilience by watching and imitating the trusted adults around them. I consider myself extremely fortunate to have had a father who modeled gratitude as a fundamental aspect of emotional resilience.

My dad, a man of quiet wisdom, didn't believe in luck. "There is no luck," he would say, "only attention, effort, and blessings." Dad reminded me of this often, as I hopped from one college major to the next, desperately seeking my calling.

When I accepted a classroom assistant position in a local Montessori school at age twenty-one, my enthusiasm was palpable. Each Saturday morning, at our weekly breakfast date, I'd recount tales from the classroom. The children's curiosity, their triumphs, the seeds of learning taking root. These stories would bring tears to Dad's eyes. "I'm proud of you, Sis," he said one day as we parted. "Your efforts are a blessing."

I carried his words close to my heart as I ventured north to Portland and later, in a leap of faith, to Dallas, Texas, for my first teaching job. In that sweltering southern heat, homesickness and doubt threatened to overwhelm me. It was then that Dad's wisdom resurfaced, not as platitude, but as practice. "Tell me about the blessings," he urged during a tearful phone call.

He shared with me a simple prayer of gratitude that had transformed his own life, inviting me to try it for myself. "Thank you, Lord, for this day. Thank you for all of my blessings." Concluding with, "Bless my efforts that they may be good, that they may be productive, and to thy glory." This ritual of attention, this daily accounting of blessings, edited slightly to make them my own, became my anchor.

Years later, as my father lay in a hospital bed, his presumed bronchitis revealed to be heart failure, the power of his philosophy shone brightest. Despite his weakened state, he welcomed a steady stream of visitors—employees, friends, family—each one expressing what he had meant to them. In those moments of connection, even as life ebbed, there was a palpable sense of blessing in the room. And as I held his hand and tearfully expressed how much I would miss him, he said, "I'll always be with you, Sis. Remember, we are blessed."

Dad's approach to life was not about blind optimism or denying hardship. Rather, it was a call to pay exquisite attention to the world around us, to recognize the intricate web of connections that sustain us, and to acknowledge the blessings that persist even in our darkest hours.

He taught me that success—in business and in life—comes from this attentive, connected way of being. His wisdom encompassed working hard, being grateful, telling the truth, joining with like-minded people, being a good steward, investing in relationships, setting clear boundaries, giving thanks daily, and striving to be a blessing to others.

In a world that often feels fractured and overwhelming, this philosophy reminds me that our smallest actions ripple outward in ways we may never know, but that matter. By cultivating awareness, recognizing our connections, and acknowledging our blessings, we weave ourselves into the fabric of something larger than our individual lives.

While gratitude doesn't stop the pain of a broken world or shield us from personal suffering, it is a way of being that fosters resilience in the face of adversity. In the end, perhaps, this is the truest form of luck—not a random stroke of fortune, but the cumulative effect of paying attention, making connections, and counting one's blessings.

Love.
Dad

A Spiral
Path

A Spiral Path

When one is feeling particularly unwell, as I have been, there is a tendency to anticipate how much worse things could be. And having experienced a few near brushes with death in my life, my mind can easily veer in that direction.

My first encounter with death occurred in tandem with Mom, during my birth, as we narrowly survived severe complications. My parents reported they nearly lost me a second time, during a seizure in infancy. But I was entirely alone during my near drowning experience at age nine, during summer camp. That one provided me with some evidence of what it might be like to die, and was my first—in memory—introduction to the still, small voice within.

The day was sunny and warm as our bus arrived at a natural rockslide, a steep sloped wall of stone and water that promised fun for those who dared. I stood behind the other children. My inability to swim was a secret I held close, a shame I couldn't voice. But peer pressure is a very real force, and soon I found myself swept into the icy steam.

As I clung to the boy in front of me, I became aware of the slick algae beneath us, the increasing speed of our descent, and shouts of excitement turning to screams of terror—my own. The world around me blurred, as I was pulled under the strong current, my arms flailing desperately.

In those moments of struggle, I suddenly felt my body relax, as if the water were holding me. The fear that had gripped me loosened its hold, while I watched vignettes of my short life played before me: my family, talking and laughing; the smell of my dog's fur, a stack of well-loved books, and the collection of treasures on my pink dresser—feathers, rocks, and dandelion wishes preserved in a jar of childhood dreams.

A warm white light beckoned and, as I drifted towards it, I felt content. At peace. I was both the observer and the observed, watching myself float towards an unknown destination.

The journey was interrupted by a deep voice: "Now is not your time…there is more for you to do." With those words, I was thrust back into the world of the living, my cheek pressed against sun-warmed stone.

In the aftermath, I found myself navigating a world that seemed both familiar and utterly changed. My ma's dismissal of my experience—"you're fine"—was a stark contrast to my gram's understanding. She listened with the patience of one who had lived long enough to know that life's most profound moments may defy explanation.

"This life is not a straight line," she told me, her fingers lightly scratching my back in a gesture of love, "but more like a spiral. The twisty parts are the hardest, but you'll be all right."

From that day at the rockslide, I became a more careful observer of life. Now, when I look back on that day, I see it less as a brush with death, and more as an invitation to live more fully. The warm, inviting light I witnessed serves as a reminder that endings can be beautiful, but it's in the spiral of life—with all its twists and turns—that we find our most profound observations and truths. And perhaps it is in these moments that we come to know ourselves better.

Sanctuary

Sanctuary

I named my home Fern Cottage, which aptly describes the peaceful, forest-like setting of this little house. Recently, though, as illness sapped my energy, chaos had begun to encroach upon my sacred space, prompting me to complain to a friend.

Her response was unexpected: "Could sanctuaries sometimes feel chaotic? Is the essence still there, even beneath the disorder?" Good questions, which have me pondering how to cultivate the art of seeing what is truly there, amidst the din and chaos of everyday life.

For me, the seed of sanctuary was planted in childhood, those formative years when we receive our first, indelible impressions of home, family, and how to move through the world—ideally, having seen a model of intention and awareness. If we're fortunate, these early lessons guide us towards a life of keen observation and connection.

My understanding of sanctuary was shaped by two powerful influences: my maternal gram and my mother. They were strong, independent women who walked in step with nature, their eyes always open to the world around them. They fed crows with the same care they might offer a guest, tended to wild creatures with observant patience. Through their watchful, playful eyes, the animals in their lives were given whimsical names and unique personality traits. The way my elders anthropomorphized animals granted us permission to see them as family.

These experiences form the bedrock of how I have come to define home—a place where attention is key, where every leaf, every visiting bird, every shift in the light is cherished.

Where do we find our personal sanctuaries? In churches? In the wildness of nature? The answer, I've come to believe through my own careful watching, is that sanctuary is something we can choose to carry with us, to create anew everywhere we find ourselves. At its core, sanctuary is a space where we are truly seen, where we connect in ways that make us feel more whole, more complete.

In the end, sanctuary is not just a physical space, but a state of being, one of acute awareness and deep presence. It's where we find ourselves reflected in the eyes of others, where we can shed our armor and simply exist, fully present in the moment. Whether it's in the company of loved ones, the solitude of nature, or the quiet corners of our own minds, sanctuary is where we come home to ourselves, where we learn to see and be seen with clarity and compassion.

As I look around Fern Cottage with renewed curiosity, I realize that even in its current state of disarray, the essence of sanctuary remains. It lives in the beauty of each fern frond, the intensity of each crow's call, and in the afternoon light streaming through the tall Douglas fir trees. The chaos, too, is part of the sacred—a reminder that life, in all its messy glory, is always worthy of our most attentive gaze.

Pumpkin Patch

Pumpkin Patch

Today would have been my mother's 89th birthday, and I'm remembering her humor, wisdom, and strength, as I ponder life's fragility. Because today, 13 years after her passing, the world feels more fragile than the day she died.

Almost a year to the day before she took her leave of this place, long before we knew anything about the cancer that was already ravaging her body, we stood in a circle of friends and family outside the mortuary where my 95-year-old grandmother's body lay. As my tears flowed, as they often do, Mom teased, "Why are you crying? She had a good long life. You should be celebrating." I stared, hoping to see a glint of sadness in her eyes, but she was unflinching. Having devoted thousands of hours of her life to visiting and ministering to those in care facilities, and organizing countless funerals, Ma had developed an irreverent attitude toward death. "*Everybody croaks!*" she would say, "*so put your attention on how you want to live.*"

One year later, as I listened to instructions from the hospice nurse, I wondered if all that unexpressed grief at having lost her parents so close together had contributed to the weakened condition of my strong mother's body. My tears again flowed freely as we sat together, my brother and I and our parents, discussing the details of my mother's illness, care, and death. She jokingly referred to me as her sensitive brown-eyed girl, and remarked that I was way more like my father than like her. That is true. But this time I could see the sadness dancing in the corners of her eyes, too.

So it should've come as no great surprise to me that in her final days, she used her last bit of strength to help me manage my grief at the loss of her.

It was October, 2011, less than a week before she died, when I came into the bedroom to find my mother propped up against her walker staring out the window at her beloved rose bushes. Even so late in the season, they were covered in blooms. I wondered if the faraway look in her eyes belied sadness, or if she was lost in the mental fog caused by the cancer pressing on her brain. "*What are you thinking, Ma?*" I inquired. "*We need a rose for that empty barrel, don't you think?*" she said, pointing to one that had stood empty for many months; an indication of her decline.

By this time she was incredibly weak and unstable on her feet, even with the walker, so I was surprised when she yelled to my dad who was resting nearby in his easy chair, "*Ole, get up! We're taking Sis to the nursery to pick out a rose!*"

Dad and I tried to talk her out of it, but she wouldn't be dissuaded. He drove and I sat in the back with Mom, whose eyes scanned the landscape along her favorite county road. *"Remember that nice farm stand, Deed?"* I nodded, recalling many times we traveled that road together in search of an estate sale, or explored the antique stores in Coburg, or walked through the pioneer cemetery. I squeezed her hand as the memories washed over me, hoping she didn't notice my tears.

At the first nursery, they told us their rose crop had been wiped out by a pest. Dad and I exchanged worried glances through the rear-view mirror. *"Drive to Bloomers, they'll have what we want!"* Mom directed. Dad had barely stopped the car in front of Bloomers Nursery when Mom flung her door open, heaved herself out of the car, and began pushing her walker across the gravel driveway. I ran ahead to clear a path. Dad followed behind, anxiously pushing his own walker over the unsteady ground and yelling, *"Sis, stop her before she falls!"*

But there was no stopping her. In what would be a final burst of energy, my mother, with her signature tenacity, hoisted her walker over a railroad tie and came to a stop in front of a bush covered in gorgeous deep orange blooms.

"*This is it, don't you think?*" she said, grinning and glancing at me for approval.

She appeared to sleep on the ride home, but as soon as Dad pulled into the driveway Ma sprung back into action, barking orders from her perch on a rickety bench: "*get my trowel from the wheelbarrow; bring that bag of garden mulch, and there's a box of bone meal in the shed; be careful as you remove her from the container, her roots are fragile; fill the hole with water and fertilizer before you put her in; take your time, don't hurry, give her roots time to settle.*"

Everything I know about roses, I learned from my mother. She'd walked me through the steps of planting, transplanting, pruning and feeding many times before. This time, though, she recited every detail as if it were the first time, though I imagine she took such care because she knew it would be the last.

Later, I came into the bedroom to find Ma once again standing at the window, peering out at the patio. "*She's a beauty, isn't she?*" she said, motioning to Pumpkin Patch. "*She's just perfect,*" I replied. "*Afterwards,*" she said, "*you'll take her home with you.*" Ma's death, despite its painful intensity, provided relatively quick passage to the next place. I did bring Pumpkin Patch home, where she stayed in the whiskey barrel on my back patio for a few years before being transplanted out front, for better sun.

For a few years, Pumpkin Patch blossomed in the most beautiful ways, always in what seemed like perfect timing, bringing vivid orange into my life. Many times, I gathered her blooms and brought them inside, put them in a vase and poured two cups of tea, one for me and one for my mom.

In the spring of 2016, without apparent cause, I walked out to find Pumpkin Patch with nondescript pale red blooms. This can happen to grafted roses that have lost the graft. There was no resemblance to the vibrant orange blossoms with which I and my mother had first fallen in love. I felt Ma's presence as sadness enveloped me, heartbroken at the loss of something that represented her love for me.

Nature doesn't stay the same, I almost heard Ma whisper. We all exist in a cycle of life and death, seasons, ever-changing landscapes, rebirth in new forms.

Perhaps my mother, in her infinite wisdom, knew that I needed that lesson as, later that same summer, I entered a long passage of chronic illness. To heal my body, I needed to offer myself the gentleness and love I had only ever extended to others. It felt foreign, like learning to write with my non-dominant hand, but my health depended on it.

This process of self-observation and awareness became crucial. Gradually, I began to recognize myself beneath the layers of pain and imperfection. My broken heart began its transformation into something stronger and more resilient. Throughout, I remembered my mother's wise guidance, to ponder how I want to live rather than wondering when I'm going to die.

Tapestry of Kinship

Tapestry of Kinship

In the tapestry of human experience, some threads may remain hidden until a gentle tug unravels the fabric of what we thought we knew. Such was the case when, at 57, I met my sister Pam for the first time.

Our mother, like so many women of her era, kept a lifelong secret about the child she had given up for adoption before meeting our father. The kind of secret that was commonplace at the time, bound by shame and unspoken love.

When Pam arrived in 1959, the record of her birth was immediately sealed in confidentiality. But she always knew of her adoption and believed that she would one day succeed in finding her birth family. Pam began to discover a lineage she never knew existed. Her journey, marked by a touch of divine synchronicity, led her to comb through microfiche records in the small coastal town where her birth mother had once lived.

She first established a lovely connection around 2013 with our dear auntie, the last of Ma's siblings, but the weight of secrecy is heavy, and she approached me, the other daughter, with the caution of one who has learned that hope can be as painful as it is powerful. Understandably, she was afraid of rejection.

It was on Mother's Day, as the world retreated into isolation because of COVID, a message arrived from Adam, Pam's son, my nephew—asking if I'd be open to meeting my sister. He reached out to me on his mama's behalf, but not with her permission—serving as a caring shield against a potential no. In that gesture, I saw the generosity of one who would risk his own heart to protect his mother's; and I knew right then, they were family.

Meeting Pam was like finding a missing piece of myself that I didn't know had been absent. Her presence as a nurse embodies a deep, instinctive care that echoes through our shared genetics. In her hands—so like our mother's, delicate yet strong—I see love etched into every line.

I often wonder what may have played out in Ma's heart each time I voiced my longing for a sister. As a mother myself, I imagine joy and sorrow, the ache of separation, the hope for a better life, the weight of an unspoken truth—all these must have wrestled within her, unbeknownst to those who loved her.

Secrets shape the landscape of lives in ways we can't always see. My brother's initial skepticism at the news of an unknown sibling stands in stark contrast to my eager acceptance, our opposite reactions evidence of the ripple effects of silence in a family.

Yet in Pam's arrival, I sensed a message from beyond—our mother's final parting gift, nine years after her departure. This was a chance for the connection she couldn't forge in life. As I reflect on the secrets harbored in my own heart, compassion wells up for the excruciatingly difficult choices Ma had faced. I've come to understand that the act of giving up a child is not a severing, but a painful stretching of love across time and space.

Pam's insight into the search for her birth family illuminates a profound truth: beyond the practical reasons lies a kind of primal need to know that one's very existence began in love. In seeking out her origins, my sister embarked on a pilgrimage to the source of her being, hoping to find that first, purest wellspring of affection.

I suspect the act of separation raged within Ma throughout her life, contributing to bouts of depression; her secret contained within a single, fragile human heart.

In the midst of a global pandemic that highlighted our human interconnectedness, our reunion felt serendipitous. I sensed our mother's invisible hand guiding us toward each other. Our unexpected kinship stands as a testament to the enduring miracle of human connection.

Today, my sister and I are on a journey of rediscovery, not just healing our own hearts, but mending a tear in the fabric of our family's narrative, weaving together the separated strands of our mother's love into a new and beautiful whole.

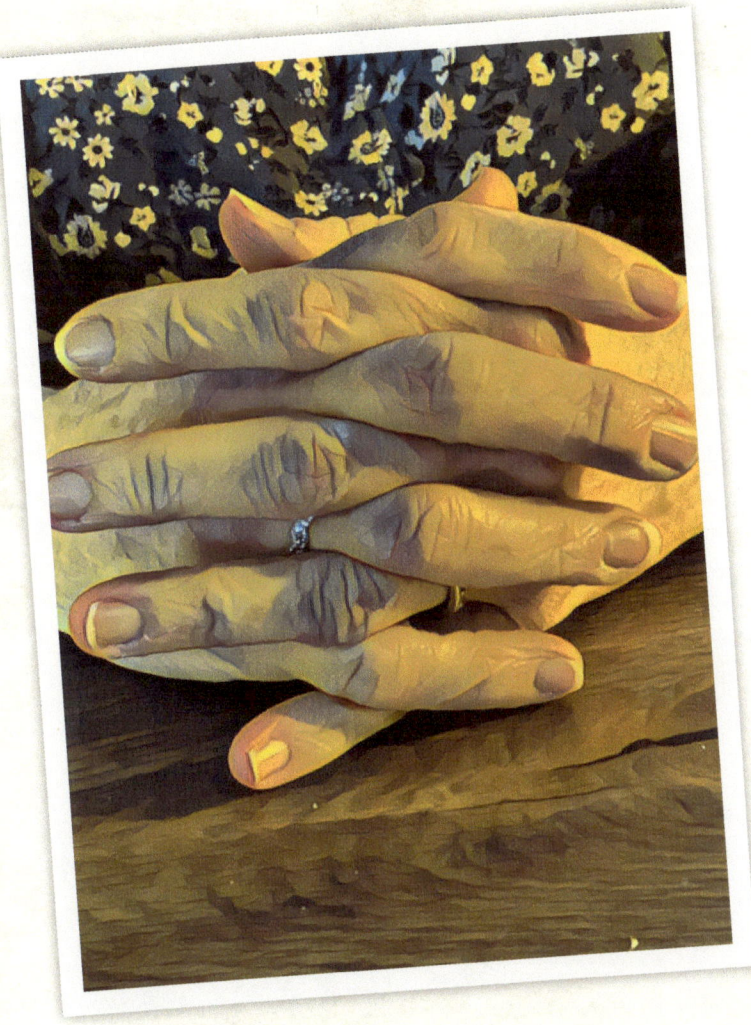

Change Can
Be Beautiful

Change Can Be Beautiful

I have been thinking a lot about the big, essential work of transformation. Flexing, bending, re-forming ourselves around ever-changing circumstances. Amidst a steady stream of news stories about the divisive, potential vicious-ness of humans, and all the ways we try to override the laws of nature, Nature herself invites us to connect with our deeper essence, the part of us that is inextricably bound to the whole web of life. The part of us that is not separate from, but innately connected to, everyone and everything else.

Every year in late summer there's a moment when every-thing shifts, a subtle revolution in the landscape that always catches my eye—and my heart—off guard. It's as if nature decides to rewrite her own story overnight. The autumn light sneaks in where summer's brilliance, just yesterday, held court, painting the world in hues of transition... and possibility.

Trees and flowers, worn from months of radiant blooming, begin to soften their stance. They tilt towards the soft light, not in defiance, but in acceptance, their leaves and petals starting to show the wear of a life fully lived. It's a slow dance of surrender, a gentle bowing to the promise of rest that lies in the rich, damp soil of the coming winter.

As I observe this annual transformation, I'm struck by how seasonal change mirrors our own human experiences of transition and resilience; of letting go and acceptance. Sometimes we reluctantly meet the inevitable shifts in our lives, bracing against the discomfort of loss, while at other times we sway and bend like leaves in preparation for the fall; innately aware that letting go is not an end, but a necessary part of our becoming.

Perhaps the sweet snuggling in of nature is a call to our own introspection, a reminder that we are part of this grand cycle. That change is growth, and growth is why we're here.

For me, this is a bittersweet moment. The melancholy isn't an emotional response to the fading summer, but a recognition of the perpetual flux of life, mine and others, which I'm feeling deeply right now. But I find hope in the shifting light that paints everything in hues of transience, reminding me that change is not just inevitable, but essential.

And in the right light, change can be very beautiful.

The Exquisite Cycle

The Exquisite Cycle

I was outside watering the garden when my neighbor, Amy, called out to me, "I have an idea for your next children's book!" She went on to tell me the beautiful tale of a little green tree frog who made its home in the watering can in her backyard. She suspected the frog was living in the bamboo, having done a bit of research about what frogs like. She sent me photos of the frog in various places doing various frog things. And the result was a delightful exchange about how we might capture the magic of this experience—perhaps this little frog would become a climate change ambassador! This was, of course, the same impetus that led me to write my first children's book, the story of Fred, the Monarch.

In the fall of 2020 a caterpillar took up residence on my dining room table, giving me a front row seat for the transformation show of a lifetime. I learned so much watching the stages of metamorphosis, against a backdrop of human-created social injustice and viral chaos. But more than anything, my time with Fred gave me a sense of companionship during the Covid lockdown. And a sense of hopefulness, that while sometimes humans are not able to be there for one another, nature is always there for us, no matter what.

I received a second milkweed plant from the same dear friend who passed along the one containing Fred. This time, it was warm enough to transplant the caterpillar into my garden. Because the wildness of nature is not as contained an environment as one's dining room table, the second caterpillar visitor did not go on to be featured in a book. In fact, after some days of chewing and growing, one morning I went out to find the one I called Frida was nowhere in sight.

I felt some sadness, of course, because the heart longs for continuance. But afterwards I thought about the beauty and purpose of feeding another being, about the utter magic of a caterpillar snatched up and swallowed into the belly of a bird or a wasp, and how that caterpillar's contribution to a healthy ecosystem supports every creature who lives there. And how only humans see ourselves as separate from that exquisite cycle.

Believing that humans, too, have the capacity to accept the temporal nature of our place in the web, I thought how fortunate I am to sit among these incredible beings, to observe their behavior and listen to the sounds of so many living things working in tandem. And to notice the ways that nature ever so subtly invites us in as an observer so that we might come to understand that we are also a participant.

This evening, I am sitting in gratitude for the blessing that is this life, yours and mine, as part of an earth community that graciously and patiently awaits our awareness and right action. May we rise to the occasion and fully embody our highest and best potential. I believe in us.

Exceptional

Exceptional

The term "exceptional" has become a respectful way to describe individuals with diverse needs and abilities. It's a fitting word, capturing the unique essence of those who navigate the world differently, inviting us to see through a more innocent lens.

In 1927, my aunt Connie was given a label we've since discarded, but today we'd recognize her neurodivergence. Connie, a year older than my father, affectionately called me "sissy." When my grandfather's sudden death plunged my grandmother into dementia, my father became Connie's guardian. Connie's emotions were pure and unfiltered, her love unconditional. She was playful, and occasionally volatile—but above all, she loved her family.

During the Democratic National Convention, when Tim Walz accepted the vice-presidential nomination, his exceptional son Gus reacted with unrestrained pride, joy, and tears. This touching moment reminded me of Aunt Connie.

Sadly, some media voices and unsympathetic observers harshly criticized Gus's open display of emotion. They turned his genuine, heartfelt response into a target for mockery.

Had Connie seen me on stage, I'm certain she would have leapt up, waving enthusiastically: "That's my sissy!" Just as Gus Walz stood tall for his father. This is the emotional foundation of healthy families: they celebrate each other without hesitation.

I was moved to tears by Walz's speech—tears of hope and relief, recognizing a politician who hadn't surrendered to cynicism. Gus Walz's reaction was a beacon of light in a week illuminated by hope for America's future.

Our nation stands at a crossroads. The path we choose will determine whether we embrace our diverse nature or succumb to division. Like seeing through Aunt Connie's eyes, we must learn to recognize the unique value in every American story. Our strength lies in this ability to understand and celebrate our differences. Of that, I feel certain.

For now, I hold onto a cautious hope: that we can reclaim an innocent perspective, one that allows us to see and cherish the diversity that makes our shared human story so exceptional.

Claudio

Claudio

I heard heartbreak defined as the natural result of opening our hearts to people and things over which we have no control.

Last January, I spent a week in Cabo San Lucas, Mexico, at a beautiful resort where a dear friend invited me to celebrate my 60th year. The place was breathtakingly beautiful, with its pristine beaches and brown pelicans diving, and whales breaching.

I met a man whose wrinkled face, broad nose, and kind eyes reminded me of my father. We interacted every day, him walking up and down the beach in the blazing sun and me, seated in my chair in the shade; the height of privilege. Eventually Claudio introduced me to his wife, Kati, who sold me a beautiful turquoise scarf. From Claudio's case, I purchased a silver rose ring, one with a Larimar stone and a sweet bracelet featuring Our Lady of Guadalupe.

In a place like Cabo, paying full price feels like an act of rebellion, though I'm sure my purchases amounted to very small drops in their very empty buckets. Which is why I gave Claudio my remaining cash on our last day. Not as a kindness, per se, but as an acknowledgment of the incredible disparity that shapes our lives.

As we were leaving I hesitantly asked Claudio for a photo, which he graciously obliged after removing his hat and smoothing his hair. As I turned to go, he said, "Thank you, my sister," words I received as the kindest I had ever heard. They were also the first English words I had heard him speak.

CS Lewis wrote, to love is to be vulnerable. Perhaps heartbreak is the very essence of being human, on the journey from here to wherever we are headed. And, perhaps, its gift is the opportunity to care deeply for whomever we meet along the way, realizing that despite our efforts to remain autonomous, we cannot hide from the fact that we belong to each other.

Wishes for America

Wishes for America

On this anniversary of September 11th, I recall that morning with absolute clarity: arriving at a friend's house, my young son in tow, only to find our friends in tears. As one quickly ushered my child into another room with the distraction of a Davy Crockett film, the other broke the news that would reshape our world. We huddled together, sobbing, fixed on the news of a nation in shock.

The terrorists who commandeered those planes, claiming thousands of lives and orphaning countless children, failed to break our spirit. In the days and months that followed, stories of unity and compassion proved America's resilience under siege. Yet now, observing the landscape of our country two decades later, I see a different kind of fracture—one that comes not from without, but from within.

Today, we face the insidious threat of fellow Americans who don the trappings of patriotism while undermining the very foundations of our democracy. They claim to understand the Constitution better than its authors, arguing for a freedom that favors the wealthy over the hard-working middle class, and demonizing immigrants like the ones who built this nation. We are a country at war with itself.

Our ability to engage in civil discourse seems to have atrophied, leaving us unable to respectfully hear differing points of view or stand witness to others' pain without judgment. When bombarded by social media soundbites and sensationalist headlines, truth can become elusive. Yet we are called to remember what happened in the past, however painful, so that we can learn from those mistakes.

In my 62nd year, I find my True North not in the blare of media-driven chaos, but in the quiet whispers of nature and the steady pulse of my own heart. As often happens in my little corner of the world, a dandelion seed drifts by on a gust of wind—a delicate ambassador of hope. I make a wish for peace and equality, then gently blow, sending it on its journey.

This moment of observation takes me back to my childhood, when I was a shy, bookish girl who preferred the company of animals to people. I would lie for hours beneath the sprawling cottonwood in our backyard, straining to catch the secret conversations of crows and squirrels. One day, the tree sent down a glistening object that alighted in my palm—a dandelion seed, my mother explained, dismissing it as a weed. But to my observant eyes, it was pure magic.

Over the years, I collected these seeds—each one a wish, a promise, a reminder of the extraordinary hidden within the ordinary. They followed me through the trials of childhood, the challenges of motherhood, and the deep grief of loss. When life's pressures threatened to crush my spirit, it was these wishes, these tangible reminders of hope, that helped me find my way back to myself.

In the heat of what may be the most consequential election in United States history, some might consider it trite to suggest that right action begins within. But I believe it to be profoundly true. As we face a world literally and metaphorically on fire, with lives lost daily to the tragedy of war and the egocentrism of humanity keeping us at odds, we must learn to observe not just with our eyes, but with our hearts.

Perhaps life is not about finding fairytale endings, but about recognizing the magic in our own stories. When we watch with quiet attention, we may come to discover the extraordinary in the ordinary, and find the strength within ourselves to face even the most daunting challenges. In this age of division and despair, our keenest observations—of ourselves, of each other, of the world around us—may be our most powerful tools for change.

In the gentle flight of the dandelion seed, I see a metaphor for hope—fragile, perhaps, but also resilient and far-reaching. And in that metaphor, I find the courage to continue observing, listening, and working towards a more peaceful future.

A Cookie for
My Inner Child

A Cookie for My Inner Child

If not for the fact that I was born on the day before my gram Lila's birthday, I would have been named Susan instead of Delila. For the first 47 years of my life, we shared almost every birthday celebration. One cake adorned with two names and a whimsical array of candles marked the 48-year gap between us.

On my 40th birthday—her 88th—we sat side-by-side in her tiny kitchen, sipping Lipton tea from the painted rooster cups that were always my favorite. With a twinkle in her eye, she leaned in close and whispered that she had something special to show me. Disappearing into one of the outbuildings, she returned with a tiny brown package tied with jute. Giggling, she handed it to me, inviting me to open it. The package was surprisingly cold to the touch.

With growing curiosity, I carefully removed the outer layer of ancient parchment paper, clearly long-preserved in the freezer. Beneath it lay a second layer of tinfoil. As I unwrapped it, I discovered a small, brown object about the diameter of a half-dollar coin, but thicker. Gram watched me intently, her awareness of my confusion evident.

Shrugging my shoulders, I admitted I had no idea what it could be. With glee, she announced, "It's a ginger snap! Your first cookie! You baked it when you were four." At that moment, I was struck by an intense wave of emotion. Here I was, holding a tiny physical representation of my childhood—a moment frozen in time through my gram's thoughtful awareness.

When I asked why she had saved it all these years, she explained, "I couldn't save the garden, but I could save the cookie you made, and I figured you might like to see it later." With a wink and a smile, she carefully rewrapped the cookie and returned it to its chilly sanctuary.

A few years later, Gram passed away at 95. At the gathering in her trailer park's community center, someone recalled how she always kept at least one angel food cake in the freezer for unexpected company. Sure enough, we found two, which we served to the guests. I took a slice, but couldn't bring myself to eat it.

That slice now rests in the far back of my freezer, wrapped in layers of tin foil and parchment paper, a lasting reminder that the work of our hands is a sacred expression of spirit, and a testament to the power of attention in preserving the moments that shape us.

Messengers
of Spirit

Messengers of Spirit

In Native traditions, as an indigenous friend once taught me, all things possess power and wisdom. A found feather is more than happenstance; it's a sacred connection between finder, bird, and the animating Spirit (God) of the universe. These delicate wings are believed to carry our prayers skyward, bridging the earthly with the divine.

Since childhood, I've been a collector of feathers—each one a testament to unseen forces at work in the world. Recently, I've gathered several crow feathers and a striking blue plume—likely from a Steller's Jay. To me, these aren't just objects, but embodiments of a legacy: a kinship with the wild passed down through generations of women in my family.

As my mother lay suspended between worlds, she whispered: "Don't forget to feed my crows!" Her words reflected a lifetime spent nurturing connections beyond the human realm. For years, crows had been her companions, gathering in expectant silence as she offered them heels of homemade bread, pizza crusts, or when times were lean, store-bought slices. These weren't acts of obligation, but rituals of communion with the untamed—a way of acknowledging our place in life's tapestry.

Even as illness ravaged Ma's body, the crows maintained their vigil. When I stepped onto the back patio of my childhood home, bread in hand, their eyes seemed to question my presence. Did they sense the impending shift? Their gaze carried the weight of an unspoken pact I wasn't sure I could honor.

My grandmother had sung to birds, coaxing them to alight on her outstretched hands—a living prayer of trust and gentleness. My young son found unexpected delight in the "good omen" of crow droppings (on my head, no less!), a story that found its way into his school report, much to his teacher's bemused surprise. These kinds of moments, seemingly trivial, are the threads from which one might weave an understanding of the world.

Do we anthropomorphize? In my family, we certainly do. And in doing so, we grant ourselves permission to forge deeper bonds with the beings that share our environment. These connections offer profound lessons in community and interdependence, inviting us into a state of continual, prayerful attention to the world around us.

When crows call overhead as I tend my garden, I pause. I listen. I look up, acknowledging their presence, while pondering their message. Sometimes, understanding arrives in a flash of insight; often, it remains elusive. But always, I remain open to the possibility of communion.

Perhaps the crows, along with the juncos, robins, and sparrows, teach us resilience in the face of an ever-changing world. Maybe they remind us to focus on the essentials: care, sustenance, shelter—the building blocks of belonging. Isn't this what we all seek? A place in existence where our calls are heard and our presence acknowledged?

A feather, then, becomes a message from the wild reminding us of what matters most. It speaks to who we are at our core: creatures longing for connection, for a sense of place in the grand, intricate web of existence.

In the end, it seems to me, we all collect tokens of the moments that shape us and the bonds that sustain us. These small treasures—feathers, memories, or daily rituals—are our prayers made manifest, anchoring us to the sacred in the everyday.

Lineage

Lineage

In some cultures and belief systems an animal or insect can represent a deceased relative, like a symbolic connection to the departed spirit—especially if the animal held significant meaning or had a strong association with the person who died.

As one who pays close attention to the symbolic messages—and messengers—that cross my path, I took notice when a juvenile dark-eyed junco landed so close to my feet.

It happened on Sunday afternoon as my sister and I stood in my driveway, in conversation—our own story of connection still unfolding. The bird danced at our feet, behaving in ways that are not typical for wild creatures. As it hopped onto my car, its gaze met ours, in what felt like a moment of shared wonderment. Then, totally bending reality, the bird alighted on my sister's head!

"I wonder if that's Yvonne?" The words escaped me before I really considered the question. My sis, who looked a bit surprised, responded, "Maybe?"

Yvonne—our mother, whom Pam never knew—had an ability to commune with creatures in a way that had once seemed eccentric to me and my friends. Now, I recognize she gave us lessons in the art of seeing a world bigger than humanity.

As we stood there, transfixed by our new feathered friend, I felt the presence of Ma—not as a ghost, but as a continuation of her teachings. She lives on in my sister and me, in the way we observe, connect, and see the world as a series of intricate relationships rather than isolated entities.

The Dance

Image is based on a photo by Rachel Hadiashar.

The Dance

A decade ago, in the harsh fluorescent light of a Nordstrom dressing room, I saw myself anew. In a rare act of self-protection, I insisted that my lover, The Conductor, wait outside as I tried on dresses for a musical gala. I couldn't bear the harshness of his criticisms.

The reflection in the mirror wasn't just of a woman trying desperately to reshape herself for a narcissist's approval; it was the image of generations of women grappling with inherited trauma. That moment of epiphany became a lens through which I began to observe the complex interplay of power, abuse, and resilience that has shaped women's lives for generations.

The personal, as always, is political. As I write this, the United States stands at a crossroads, with women's rights under siege. The overturning of Roe v. Wade, the persistent gender pay gap, and the alarming rates of domestic violence, all stem from the same root: a society that has normalized the subjugation of women.

The narcissistic manipulation tactics I experienced in that dressing room are not so far removed from the gaslighting we witness on the national stage, where male politicians who claim to respect women and promise to protect our rights are systematically dismantling them. All while blatantly attempting to silence us.

Not long ago, I encountered the familiar dance of abuse and gaslighting in a professional setting. A 40-something attorney, reminiscent of my past tormentor, launched into a relentless monologue posing as conversation, a thinly veiled attempt to overpower and get his way. This time, I saw through the manipulation more quickly and disengaged.

Pattern-breaking takes practice, given how deeply we, as women, have normalized such treatment in our homes and workplaces.

The #MeToo movement brought these issues into sharper focus, catalyzing a moment in American history where change ripples in a groundswell of collective refusal. A chorus of voices rises to say, "Enough!" This awakening has the potential to shift our societal consciousness, but it requires more than just recognizing manipulation. It demands that we question why we, as a society, have come to accept self-absorption, dominance, and extraversion as qualities of leadership.

In this current moment, we are seeing women step into unprecedented positions of power, yet the backlash against this progress is fierce. The vitriol directed at female politicians, journalists, and activists is a testament to the deep-seated fear of women's empowerment. It's a reflection of a culture devoted to tearing women down and then selling us potions and pills and gadgets to build us back up.

Recognizing manipulation is the first step, but it takes time and practice to reject deep-seated messages of unworthiness and replace them with self-acceptance. With awareness comes the possibility of collective awakening—one widespread enough to fortify the democratic ideals of equality against the erosive force of unchecked power.

Women standing together at this juncture are challenging the very systems that have allowed narcissism and misogyny to thrive. It's a reclamation of space, of voice, of the right to exist without constant negation. In this act of collective resistance, we glimpse the possibility of a world where narcissistic manipulation and gaslighting are recognized, named, and firmly rejected.

As we approach another pivotal election, the power of observation extends far beyond recognizing manipulation in our personal lives. It's about seeing clearly the tactics used to undermine women's rights and autonomy in the political sphere. It's about understanding our collective worth and recognizing the strength that lies in our shared experiences.

While narcissism isn't vanishing, its inevitability in our lives is being questioned. We're realizing that while we can't eradicate the condition, we can choose not to elevate egomaniacs to positions of power, not to intertwine our lives with theirs, not to grant them the intimacy of friendship or the sanctity of our inner circles.

We aren't going back. Instead, we're moving forward, eyes wide open, observing the dance we've been taught and choosing to create new steps that celebrate the strength and beauty of every person's journey. This new dance is rooted in keen observation, self-awareness, and the courage to challenge longstanding norms with a strong and resounding, "No!" It's rooted in camaraderie and community.

The trauma lives in our bodies. Women who have survived narcissist abuse feel the weight of re-traumatization as we watch a predatory man and his enablers vie for our nation's highest office. For those of us fortunate to emerge from those entanglements, it was often friends who recognized the abuse and refused to defend the abuser, who helped us find solid ground again.

In this moment of political upheaval and social reckoning, we have the opportunity to break free from the chains of generational trauma and create a new narrative. One where we are not defined by the manipulations we've endured, but by the resilience and wisdom we've gained in overcoming them.

It's time to turn our collective gaze toward a future where empathy, compassion, and nurturance are recognized as the true foundations of leadership and societal progress. Together, we possess the collective power to wage this, the most crucial fight of our lives. Our unity is their greatest fear. Community is our greatest strength.

It's time.

Good
Vibrations

Good Vibrations

A year ago, a beekeeper friend posed an unexpected question: would you like to host a hive at Fern Cottage? The proposition felt both daunting and intriguing, much like the bees—small yet mighty, gentle yet fierce.

Six months later, she called to say the time had come. My son and I drove in darkness to help relocate a colony of slumbering bees to their new home, my heart thrumming with anticipation—and a wee bit of fear!

Kelly, the beekeeper, trained by years of careful observation, had already scanned the landscape for the ideal location. She considered several factors: morning sun to warm the hive, afternoon shade to prevent overheating, and protection from prevailing winds. In what I consider to be a divine stroke of serendipity, the perfect spot emerged just beyond the wall of my bedroom.

Sleeping near bees, I've discovered, is nothing short of enchanting. Some will dismiss this notion, but I'm convinced I can sense their collective vibration through the wall barrier. My dreams have taken on a new quality. The bees' presence has awakened something profound on this land—something that transcends pollination and honey production.

There's an energy about honey bees that draws me outside and compels me to observe. On sweltering days of summer, I watched in fascination as they engaged in a behavior called "bearding"—clustering together outside the hive entrance in a living, breathing mass. This remarkable act of cooperation helps regulate the internal temperature, crucial for the developing brood and the integrity of the wax combs within.

Bees give us a model for a society of astonishing complexity and altruism. When a worker bee senses its imminent death, it leaves the hive. This final act of selflessness ensures that its sisters won't need to expend precious energy removing its lifeless body, a task that would divert resources from the ceaseless work of the colony.

The longer I listen, the more I recognize the subtlety in their communication. The bees' sounds shift in pitch and intensity. Using a complex system of pheromones, dance, and vibrations, they share information about food sources, threats, and the overall state of the colony. When a curious observer—human or animal—lingers too long at the hive entrance, the bees' tone changes unmistakably. It's a clear message: "Step back!"

A friend helped me move an old garden table into position for optimal hive viewing at a reasonable distance. Observing the bees became a regular daily activity during this summer of reflection and healing. In the months since their arrival, I've come to see the bees as teachers, demonstrating the power of cooperation, the beauty of purpose, and the profound interconnectedness of all living things.

Reflections on Reverence

Reflections on Reverence

For decades, my family participated in an annual sacred ritual the day before Memorial Day at Willamette National Cemetery. We gathered to honor our beloved departed, our attention focused on a sea of flags stretching to the horizon, each placed by children's hands in remembrance of sacrifices most of us cannot imagine. With reverence, we decorated their gravestones with flowers from our gardens—peonies for grandfather Elliott, bearded iris for grandmother Florence, roses for other family friends nearby. These offerings symbolized our gratitude for their service to a purpose greater than family or self, connecting us to their memory and the values they upheld.

In those not-so-distant days, we naively believed threats to our democracy came only from foreign shores. How unprepared we were for the storm brewing within our own borders! Our ancestors could never have foreseen that the greatest threat to our democratic experiment would emerge from the very party they once supported and believed supported them.

Now, we observe with growing alarm how violence and intimidation have become normalized, severing the connections that once bound us as a nation. Recently at Arlington

Cemetery, thugs accompanying a former president physically assaulted a worker who, while fearing for her safety, chose not to press charges. This incident starkly illustrates the state of our nation: a place where those tending the graves of heroes face bullying from followers of a would-be dictator. Even election workers are resigning en masse, fearing retaliation from right-wing extremists.

Sadly, some Americans embrace fear as a platform, even echoing the violent rhetoric of an unhinged leader.

Our greatest democratic tool—our vote—suddenly feels fragile, threatened by those who don't actually believe in liberty and justice for all. During this time when I myself am challenged to get out of bed in the morning, it's hard to think about becoming a revolutionary in defense of democracy. And yet, forces bigger than all of us seek to divide us. Gigantic media companies profit from the drama created by politicians who seek power and corporate dictatorship.

We, the people, are on the outside of this vicious cycle, our attention pulled in different directions, weakening the connections that once united us. We can and we must take a stand for what is right. But in doing so, we must not forget our compassion. We must not sacrifice the relationships that are dear to us, simply because we cannot find the words to connect. If we remain passive, we risk losing the dream of freedom for which so many have fought and died. If we sacrifice relationships at the altar of righteousness, we lose something even more important: our humanity.

As we face these challenges, let us remember the attention and care we once devoted to honoring our fallen heroes. May we now turn that same level of attention to preserving the relationships we hold dear.

A Rose of
Imperfection

A Rose of Imperfection

I love the wild unruliness of my native landscape and what it teaches me about the beauty of aging and evolving, imperfectly.

If I could embody a plant, I think I would choose the Nootka Rose—a wild beauty that defies convention. In early summer, she offers a fleeting profusion of delicate pink petals, and she grows even more beautiful from there. In fact, I find her near-autumn guise most captivating with rose hips of crimson.

As the season progresses, these hips evolve, their skins puckering like the faces of elders. Nootka Rose grows more arresting with time. Her fruit, once smooth and bright, now bears the textured wisdom of age—each wrinkle a testament to endurance, each deepening hue a celebration of maturity.

In this metamorphosis, the Nootka Rose offers a timely reminder: true beauty is not static, nor is it bound to the fleeting blush of youth. Rather, it is a dynamic force, one that gathers potency through the accumulation of days, the weathering of seasons, the quiet persistence of being.

Year after year, I plan to harvest those gorgeous fruits for winter tea, but I can't bring myself to pluck them. Her magnificence transcends utility and is best enjoyed in the garden.

Our Lady of
Fern Cottage

Our Lady of Fern Cottage

In my most uncomfortable moments of illness, I sometimes find myself yearning for the kind of care I received from my mother and grandmother. Their nurturing hands, the comforting alchemy of their cooking, the gentle back scratches, and their uproarious laughter—all vivid again in my mind's eye. That sweet sort of attention that conveys a deep sense of safety and love's certainty.

Another mother, Mary, has held a fascination for me since I first glimpsed Our Lady of Guadalupe in stained glass, catching the light in a Catholic sanctuary. When I asked Mom about her, she replied with characteristic irreverence, "She was Jesus' mother," in a tone that indicated hers was a somehow lesser role in that famous story.

Like most Scandinavians, I grew up attending Lutheran Church. Fortunately, ours was one of the more liberal varieties where love, acceptance, inclusion, and service were the fundamental tenets. My mother was devout in her Christian faith. She walked that talk, dedicating her life to service. Whether communing with elders in nursing homes or children in schools, she poured her heart and her time into helping others.

Ma was also a slightly contemptuous woman who straddled worlds, firmly rooted in her generation's patriarchal norms and a believer in magic. This duality allowed her to see the extraordinary in the ordinary, to find connection in unexpected places. Perhaps this is why, decades later, when Our Lady of Guadalupe appeared as an apparition on my dining room wall, I could almost hear my mother's voice calling me "kooky"—with a hint of wonder in her tone.

The appearance of Mary in my little cottage, surrounded by a cathedral of Doug Fir trees, birdsong, and the hum of bees, felt like a visitation from the great mother herself. Not in a Catholic way, but as a manifestation of a more universal maternal energy. She is Mother Nature, every nurturer who has ever tended to the needs of children, animals, countries, and continents. She is the attention that shapes the world.

In that moment of apparition, when I needed encouragement, I chose to believe. Could it have been a trick of light, a strange refraction through the dining room window? Possibly. But in the absence of a mundane explanation, I embraced the extraordinary. I saw it as a mother showing up on my wall when my own couldn't be there, a compassionate presence bridging the gap between the tangible and the divine.

Perhaps such a visitation speaks to our deep human need for connection, our desire to be seen and nurtured. Whether we find it in the arms of our mothers, in the face of a saint, or in the play of light on a dining room wall, we are constantly seeking that attentive gaze that says, "I see you. You matter."

It's a reminder that care and attention can come from unexpected sources, that the universe itself might bend its gaze toward us in moments of need.

In the end, it matters less whether the apparition was "real" in a scientific sense. What matters is the connection it fostered, the attention it demanded, and the comfort it provided. In choosing to believe, I opened myself to a larger web of care—one that extends from the most personal memories of my mother's love to the vast, impersonal forces of nature that sustain us all. Within that web, I find home.

Image is based on a felted Guadalupe by artist,
Rosa Guadalupe Vela Sachs.

Grace

Grace

What we perceive as sacrifice, nature recognizes as cycle. This truth echoes through the seasons, relationships, and life itself—a recurring theme in these summer reflections. Our wise animal teachers offer lessons in fluidity, guiding us through life's ebbs and flows with grace and resilience.

One such teacher, a beautiful Dark-eyed Junco, etched herself into my heart a few summers ago. Her gentle clicks came through my screen door, drawing my attention to her nest-building in a basket partially concealed by a blooming camellia. I stood transfixed, observing her meticulous work, attempting to mimic her clicks in my clumsy way.

One morning, the absence of her familiar song prompted me to investigate. As I opened the screen door, she darted out, alighting on a nearby boxwood. Her frantic clicks filled the air as I peeked inside to discover eggs! In the days that followed, I tried to balance curiosity with respect, offering Mama the quiet she needed.

Many days later, Mama Junco's watchful gaze followed me from her camellia perch as I approached, her soft, syncopated trill inviting me closer. In a dance of trust, she hopped close, then flew to the basket's edge. Our eyes met for a moment before she peeked into her nest and retreated to the camellia. Taking her cue, I peered inside to find a wiggly mass of closed eyes, tiny beaks, and downy fuzz—she was showing me her babies!

For days, in a flurry of maternal devotion, Mama Junco tirelessly flew in and out, feeding her tiny, screeching brood. But nature's cycles can be cruel as well as beautiful. One night, a loud thud shattered the peace, and I discovered a neighborhood cat poised beneath the basket. Though I shooed the intruder away, Mama Junco had vanished.

While not surprised, the next morning I felt utterly heartbroken to discover four tiny, still bodies in the nest. Beneath a towering Doug Fir outside my front door, I laid the babies to rest among other beloved creatures, adorning their grave with a camellia bloom and a feather—perhaps their mother's—found nearby.

I felt thankful the babies had passed together in their cozy nest, rather than in the jaws of a cat. And I honored Mama Junco, whose presence and attention had graced my doorstep and touched my heart.

This encounter taught me a profound lesson in acceptance. In her brief time nesting in the shade of Fern Cottage, Mama Junco showed me how to pay attention to the small miracles unfolding around us. In the face of nature's cycles—beautiful and brutal alike—we may find our own capacity for grace. God bless the wild teachers who, if we listen closely, help us navigate the intricate dance of existence.

Remembering
Who I Am

Remembering Who I Am

Every autumn, melancholy arrives unannounced, like a fog slowly descending. It creeps in with the changing season, revealing itself through weeks of interrupted sleep, intense dreams, and spontaneous tears. Only then do I realize: oh, it's almost October. My body remembers.

In a three-year span between 2008 and 2011, October became a month of loss, claiming three beloved members of my family of origin. Gramp passed first, two years later Gram followed, and exactly a year later, Ma took her leave. Now, as the leaves turn and the air cools, my senses awaken not only to the beauty of the season, but also to the deep grief that lingers in its shadows.

Autumn was their favorite season, as it is mine—a shared love that bridges the gap between worlds. I recall my grandparents' joy during their autumn drives to, as Gram would say, "see the leaves." We'd collect the most colorful specimens, sending them back and forth in the mail, a ritual of connection across distances. Once, my mother even shipped autumn leaves all the way to Texas, gifting my first group of Montessori students a glimpse of my homeplace—a gesture that proves her nurturing spirit.

In one particularly challenging autumn, weighed down by circumstance, I opened a box of memorabilia. Out tumbled a message from my mother, sent decades ago with her characteristic blend of love and humor. This woman, who daily consulted both her Bible and her horoscope, reminded me of the qualities associated with my Chinese zodiac sign: peaceful, attentive, smart, artistic, resourceful—a rabbit. Ma, a woman of both faith and mysticism, reached across the veil with words I needed to hear, proving that wisdom can arrive in unexpected packages.

If we think of souls as travelers weaving through the cycles of a universe we can never fully understand, perhaps those we hold dear are never truly gone. They become part of the fabric of our existence, their essence infused in the changing leaves, the crisp air, and the memories that surface in perfect timing.

As we navigate seasons of life, of joyful renewal, loss, and remembrance, may we acknowledge the moments and memories that tether us to the precious souls who have shaped us. This way, we can honor not just their absence, but the enduring presence of their wisdom and humor.

In this season of transition, I find solace in the cyclical nature of life. Grief is a testament to the beauty I've witnessed and the love I've shared. It connects me to the larger story of lives intertwined across generations and seasons. It helps me remember who I am.

Gathering &
Letting Go

Gathering & Letting Go

22 September, 2024

Today is the autumnal equinox, a good day to think about what we want to gather in the coming year, and what is ready to be released. This year I aim to release inflammation—of body, mind, and spirit—and gather in the blessings of connection.

It is a good day to complete this collection that honors mine as a small part of a much bigger story. If you've come this far with me, I implore you: write your own story. In a world hungry for our attention, your stories are a beacon.

In Montessori education, we hold in highest esteem the everyday stories we share with children and each other. Because true life stories are more captivating than any fiction, as you've surely noticed when sharing a real life event with a young listener. The garden and the grocery store become realms of wonder, not because they're extraordinary, but because they involve us—living, stumbling, rising, and finding meaning in the seemingly mundane. Through these stories, we demonstrate how the simple act of paying attention becomes an essential element in a life well lived.

We may not exit this life in the arms of those we cherish, but we will leave behind the essence of what made us beloved and remembered. Our experiences, joys, disappointments, loves, and losses remain as energetic imprints on the hearts of those who knew and loved us.

Your attention to my stories is a gift. Now, I eagerly await yours. In sharing the moments that make up our lives, we illuminate the interconnected web of human experience. Each story told is an act of resistance against the inattention that threatens to dim our collective light.

With gratitude for your presence and attention,

Delila

Autumn
Haiku

gentle shimmering

in the shade of Cedar tree

hope is a Mollusk

Author Bio

Delila Olsson's roots run deep in the forests of the Pacific Northwest. A native Oregonian, she has spent her life cultivating growth—in children, gardens, and herself. Her journey as an Montessori educator has been marked by a passion for nurturing potential and fostering connection.

Delila's first book, "*Fred the Monarch: A Tale of Transformation and Hope*," emerged during the pandemic, teaching her to slow down and witness the magic all around us. It's a story about finding wonder in unexpected places.

When not writing or guiding educational initiatives, Delila can be found wandering on forest trails, tending her garden, or curled up in her Lake Oswego cottage with a good book. She shares her home with Staccato, the cat, and Rocky, the dog, and her heart with Elliott, her son.

www.ingramcontent.com/pod-product-compliance
Lightning Source LLC
Chambersburg PA
CBHW040851120626
46547CB00006B/569